Dedicated to my students,
- Mrs. Dorcely

This book belongs to:

_____

At the sports camp,

There is a soccer field.

I see a soccer ball.

I see a soccer net.

There is a baseball field.

I see baseball bats.

I see a baseball.

There is a volleyball court.

I see a volleyball net.

I see a volleyball.

There is a bowling alley.

I see the bowling pins.

I see a bowling ball.

There is a running area.

I see a track and field.

**I see a ball and spoon
relay race.**

There is a field hockey pitch.

I see a hockey net.

I see a field hockey stick.

I see a hockey ball.

There is a dance studio.

I see barres.

There is a gymnastics area.

I see beams.

There is a basketball court.

I see a basketball hoop and net.

I see a basketball.

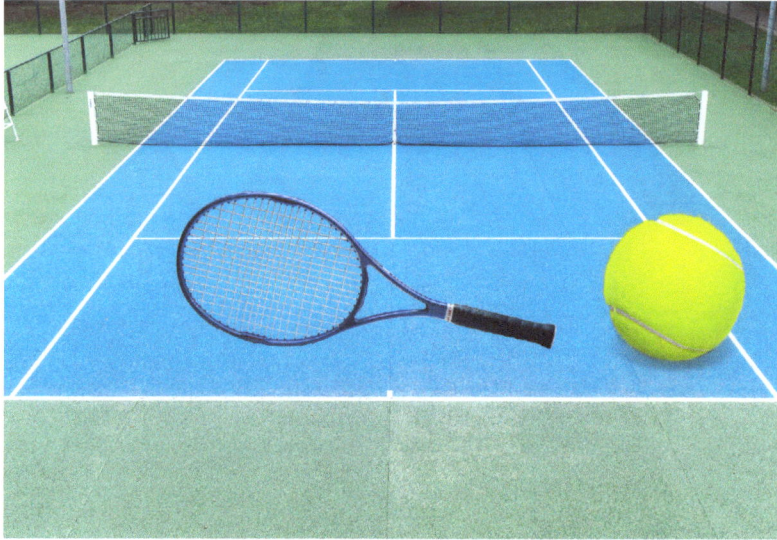

There is a tennis court.

I see tennis rackets.

I see tennis balls.

I see a tennis net.

There is a golf course.

I see golf clubs.

I see golf balls.

There is a cycling area.

I see bicycles.

I see helmets.

There is a swimming area.

I see a swimming pool.

I see an inner tube.

At last, I see a snack area.

The Sports Camp

ball

baseball bat

basketball hoop

bicycle

 **bowling pin**

 **golf club**

 **helmet**

 **swimming pool**

 **inner tube**

net

racket

snack

track

www.ingramcontent.com/pod-product-compliance
Lightning Source LLC
LaVergne TN
LVHW072054070426
835508LV00002B/84